Subtle Beauty in the Winter's Glow

On icy branches, ice cream sticks,
Little fairies dance, pulling tricks.
They giggle softly, whisper and spin,
In this chilly realm, let the fun begin.

Snowflakes tumble like silly hats,
Falling down on lazy cats.
The trees chuckle, swaying low,
While snowmen's noses steal the show.

A slippery slide for the squirrel to take,
Zooming down without a break.
Hot cocoa spills, laughter erupts,
Even the icicles are slightly uptight.

The world turns bright with magic's glow,
As every frost inspires a new flow.
With each chilly giggle, the winter does sway,
In this playful dance, we all want to play.

Original title:
Frosted Fern Fantasies

Copyright © 2025 Creative Arts Management OÜ
All rights reserved.

Author: Christian Leclair
ISBN HARDBACK: 978-1-80566-722-3
ISBN PAPERBACK: 978-1-80566-851-0

The Secret Patterns of the Frost

A canvas white where patterns tease,
Twirling tales on the icy breeze.
Each inch a story, each flake a grin,
Frost whispers loudly, let the fun begin.

The flowered frost draws a silly face,
Making winter feel like a dance party place.
"With every shiver, don't hold back your cheer,
For even the snowflakes have giggles here!"

In the morning light, all shapes combine,
A jigsaw puzzle made divine.
"Who knew the chill could bring such delight?
Let's twirl with the frost till the end of the night!"

Secrets lie in a frost-covered maze,
As tiny footprints leave their praise.
Patterns unfold in a whimsical sprawl,
"Join the fun, it's a frost fairy ball!"

Celestial Ferns of the North

In slippers made of snow, they dance,
Each frond a star, they take a chance.
With giggles soft, they twirl and hop,
In chilly swirls, they never stop.

The moon peeks through, all wide-eyed,
As ferns do cartwheels, full of pride.
They throw a party, invite the breeze,
And sip on dew from frosted trees.

Tempest of Frozen Reveries

A blizzard comes, the ferns are bold,
They tell tales of ice, brash and bold.
With whispers of winter, they strut about,
Creating legends, without a doubt.

They wear tiny hats made of snowflakes,
And laugh so hard, the icicles shake.
In this frozen realm, mischief reigns,
As ferns play tricks, ignoring refrains.

Secrets in the Shards of Ice

In crystal caves where secrets hide,
Ferns tell jokes that are wild and wide.
With glimmers of frost upon their lips,
They burst out laughing during ice trips.

A pun or two from each shimmering blade,
Makes snowmen giggle, completely swayed.
The chilly air is filled with cheer,
As ferns exchange gags with a frosty leer.

Lullabies of the Winter Wood

In the stillness, where shadows lay,
Ferns hum tunes that dance and sway.
Their lullabies tickle the trees,
With whispering winds and glistening freeze.

Underneath the moon's soft wink,
They swap tales while the world thinks.
Their laughter echoes through the night,
In the winter wood, all is light.

Ethereal Patterns in the Snow

In the chill, the patterns twist,
Snowflakes dance, a frosty mist.
Snowmen giggle, hats askew,
Making snowballs just for you.

Icicles hang like frozen swords,
Squirrels in coats playfully hoard.
Snow angels with wings so grand,
Leave behind a soft, cold land.

Crystalline Forests of Whimsy

Wandering through a glittering maze,
Where trees wear coats in snowy rays.
Bizarre creatures peek and play,
In this winter wonderland ballet.

A pickle-shaped snowman stands tall,
With a tap-dancing hat, he enthralls.
Penguins slide on slippery slopes,
While weaves of frost fill our hopes.

Glistening Leaves of the Enchanted Grove

Leaves dazzle in the winter light,
Squirrels debate who'll fly a kite.
Giggles echo beneath the bough,
Those leaves would laugh, if they knew how!

Fairies throw snowball fights so grand,
Twirling in their sparkly band.
With each splat, a chorus sings,
Winter's joy, oh what it brings!

The Secret Life of Winter's Art

Little critters in scarves of white,
Conspire under the pale moonlight.
Canvas of snow, their giggling spree,
Painting the ground with glee, oh me!

Here comes a bear, slipping with flair,
As snowballs fly through icy air.
Turtles in hats stroll without care,
Winter silliness everywhere!

Shimmers in the Chilly Light

In the chilly morn, the green leaves shiver,
They wear icy coats, looking to deliver.
Giggles of frost dance on every flake,
While drowsy squirrels awake, make no mistake.

The grass whispers jokes, in a frosty attire,
Tickling toes, like a naughty wire.
Even the shadows walk with a bounce,
As snowflakes twirl, they flit and pounce.

Beneath a Glassy Canopy

Beneath the shiny roof, the world looks grand,
A slippery floor, oh, isn't it planned?
Chasing the sunlight, the giggles ensue,
Skating on puddles, just me and my shoe.

Pinecones are chuckling, the branches sway,
While icicles dangle in a silly display.
All nature laughs in rhymes, oh what glee,
In this frosty realm where we all want to be.

Frozen Rhapsody in the Meadow

In the meadow of dreams, the laughter does rise,
Each little twig dons the frosty disguise.
As rabbits perform in their white-gloved show,
They leap and prance, creating quite a glow.

The snowman's got moves, he spins with delight,
Dancing with shadows till the fall of night.
Chortles erupt from the ice-covered brooks,
With fish exchanging their giggling looks.

Sylvan Dreams in Silver Haze

In the woods where the silver mist plays pretend,
Trees gossip sweet nothings as branches extend.
Every hushed murmur is wrapped in a grin,
While deer crack up, trying not to give in.

A mishap with snow, a tumble unwound,
A raccoon rolls over, to laughter he's bound.
With each frosty breath, the fun just amps high,
Under the moon, as the owls hoot a sigh.

Chills in the Velvet Twilight

When night falls in a velvet hue,
The trees wear coats of sparkling dew.
The rabbits jump, they twirl and spin,
While squirrels juggle acorns, grinning like kin.

A chill in the air, a tickle on the nose,
As penguins slide down slopes in rows.
A snowman coughs, he's lost his hat,
While nearby, a bear does a silly prat.

Diamond Dawn on the Glade

Morning breaks with a bling and a spark,
While gnomes have tea and dogs play fetch in the park.
Snowflakes disco in the sunlight's gleam,
As wise old owls plot a funnier scheme.

The trees giggle as the sun winks wide,
While snowflakes pirouette, taking joy in the ride.
A frosty boot slips, oh what a sight,
As a lumberjack dances, wrapped up tight.

Spheres of Snowlight and Shadow

Bouncing balls of snow collected with glee,
Bring laughter and shouts from a bright jubilee.
A cat pounces, but the ball rolls away,
While kids toss snowballs, oh what a display!

Laughter echoes through the frosty glow,
As gophers pop up to say hello.
A snow-covered hill becomes a slide,
Where giggles and squeals can't be denied.

The Frost-kissed Elegy

A song of the icy, a ballad of cheer,
Where penguins strut with a flair sincere.
The moon takes a bow, all shy and sweet,
As ice skaters twirl on the shimmering street.

Frosty air makes noses red,
While wise cracks from trolls play in our heads.
A snowflake slips on a banana peel,
Creating a spectacle, oh what a reel!

Whispers of Icy Veils

In the garden, sneaky snowflakes play,
Hiding where the daisies sway.
A squirrel slips on a frosty patch,
Lands in a snowdrift with a splash!

Giggling trees don their icy attire,
Mimicking dancers around a fire.
A rabbit hops in a sparkly coat,
And joins in with a giggly note.

Frosty giggles, they twist and twirl,
As icicles dangle and whirl.
Each breath a cloud in the chilly air,
While the moon laughs from its lair.

What a silly winter soirée tonight,
With chuckles echoing in pure delight.
The frosty veil shimmers with glee,
In this wintry comedy, oh so free!

Enchanted Frosted Dreams

On a hilltop glistens pure white foam,
A penguin slides, claiming it home.
He trips over snow, falls down with flair,
And laughs as he rolls without a care!

Tiny snowflakes, like jesters, swirl,
Tickling noses of every girl.
In the night, they put on a show,
With icy pirouettes in a frosty glow.

A snowman's carrot, a tiny pretzel twist,
In an outfit that you can't resist.
With buttons scattered, he attempts a pose,
Only to topple, just like his nose!

As stars wink down on this frigid scene,
The laughter echoes, crisp and keen.
In enchanted dreams, all frolic and play,
With joy in the air, come what may!

Delicate Crystals in the Moonlight

Beneath the stars, in a wondrous glow,
Dewdrops twinkle on the frost below.
A cat prances, all poofy and proud,
But slips on ice, ending her crowd!

With sparkles dancing on every bite,
Snowflakes gather for a midnight bite.
A horse in boots, wearing shades of blue,
Struts like a star, waving woo-hoo!

All around, winter jokes and glee,
As snowflakes whisper, 'Join us, you see?'
In this crystal landscape, mirth blooms bright,
With giggles that sparkle in the moonlight.

What fun we'll have in this snowy spree,
With laughter lifting us unreservedly.
For under the chill of this winter's reign,
Joy and laughter will always remain!

Echoes of Winter's Breath

In a snowy realm where whispers play,
The wind tells jokes to the trees each day.
A bear in a scarf, looking quite grand,
Skids on ice, falling down just as planned!

Icicles dangle, like prizes on high,
As munching mice, in a frozen pie.
They nibble and giggle with every bite,
While snowflakes join them, dancing in flight.

By the frosty lake, a natty raccoon,
Juggles snowballs under the moon.
He slips and goes splat, what a fine show,
Springing up laughing with an elegant bow!

Laughter echoes in the winter's breath,
Fetching joys with each frosty step.
A comical tale, in this chilly contest,
Where fun and giggles stand out the best!

Reflections in the Frosted Glass

In the morning chill, I see my face,
Trapped in a glass, my winter embrace.
My hair's a frosty stand of ice,
Oh, how I wish for a summer slice!

A mug of cocoa warms my hands,
As snowflakes dance and make their plans.
I laugh at squirrels with tiny hats,
Waging war on playful cats!

The window's art is quite surreal,
A frozen world that's hard to feel.
I sip my drink, a winter perk,
Wondering how penguins do this work!

The sun will shine, it's just a tease,
A glint of hope in icy breeze.
I'll bust a move, like an ice-skate pro,
Through this frosty fun, let's go, let's go!

The Quiet Elegy of Cold

The grass wears frost like a fancy gown,
Nature's pranks make winter frown.
I tried to skate, but I fell instead,
Now I sit, with snow on my head!

A whisper comes from trees so bare,
They giggle softly, as snowflakes stare.
The crunch beneath my boots, what fun!
They laugh and tease, 'Let's run, let's run!'

Hot cocoa spills from a cup so wide,
As I chase snowflakes that quickly hide.
Each snowman formed just might get shy,
With carrots lost to a hungry guy!

While icicles dangle like frozen teeth,
They risk a plunge with every breath.
A winter tale, with laughter unrolled,
In the quiet dark, our giggles unfold.

Timeless Beauty in Winter's Grasp

The world's a canvas, painted white,
With little critters prepared for flight.
Braving the cold, they scamper along,
With sweaters on, they feel so strong!

I bundled up, looking quite the sight,
A marshmallow puff in morning light.
The dog runs wild, a furry blur,
Rolling in snow, a snowy stir!

Mittens lost, and scarves awry,
As snowstorms swirl, I can't help but cry.
I'll dance on ice, like a bold jazz fan,
While winter catches me unplanned!

With jokes and laughter, I claim the day,
Through snowy fields, I twist and sway.
Winter, you sly, humorous chap,
Let's toast to you with a warm flapjack!

Fractal Patterns of Icy Whimsy

In the forest deep, the branches play,
With icy crystals that just won't stay.
I try to catch them, quick as a fox,
But they giggle and flee like crafty rocks!

The trees are dressed for a winter fête,
With sparkling snow, they're feeling great.
But a squirrel steals the show, I swear,
As he plays peekaboo, without a care!

I start to drift on a pond of glass,
With flailing limbs, oh what a gas!
A winter's waltz, complete with spills,
Every tumble brings more thrills!

With whispers of laughter among the pines,
Nature's jokes become our signs.
Embrace the chill, let's seize this chance,
For whimsical frosts, let's dance, let's dance!

Enchantment of the Snowbound Grove

In a grove where snowflakes play,
The trees wear coats of white ballet.
A squirrel slips and makes a fuss,
'Who needs a gym? This snow's our bus!'

Chubby rabbits hop and freeze,
In suits of white, they sneak with ease.
A snowball fight, they start to scheme,
Whipping fluff like it's a dream.

The owls chuckle from their perch,
As little birds begin to lurch.
With frosted wings, they glide and swoop,
In the frostwork, they form a group.

So here's to giggles in the cold,
Snowmen sprout, both brave and bold.
The wonders of this winter spree,
Make any heart skip with glee!

The Airy Touch of Winter's Whisper

A gentle breeze in crisp white fluff,
Whispers of cold and stuffy gruff.
The trees giggle and bend their knees,
While icicles laugh, 'We're sure a tease!'

Under snow, the flowers sigh,
'Why'd we sleep? Oh me, oh my!'
Yet snowflakes dance like tipsy sprites,
In the moonlight, they hold light fights.

A penguin waddles, takes a bow,
With sliding grace, he'll show us how.
The whole world seems to shimmy and shake,
'Who knew that winter's ice could break?'

So let's embrace this frosty chill,
With laughter's warmth, we'll have our fill.
In winter's charm, we find delight,
With goofy antics, all feels right!

Glacial Whirls in the Moonlight

Under the stars, the ice does twirl,
As frigid winds start to unfurl.
The moon attempts its best to glow,
While chilly ghosts make shadows grow.

A polar bear gives quite the show,
Slipping down a hill of snow.
'Watch me glide!' he calls in glee,
While snowflakes drift so carelessly.

The owls hoot, a comical crew,
Swapping jokes about the view.
They argue where the best spots are,
As frostbitten critters trade their bar.

In frosty realms of icy night,
We find a dance, a wondrous sight.
With each swirl and each merry spin,
The frosted world invites the grin!

Crystal Lattice of Nature's Art

In nature's studio, crisp and bright,
Ice sculptures formed by morning light.
The trees wear lace like frosty covers,
While woodpeckers dance with their blunders.

Each twig a canvas, each leaf a tale,
Where skaters glide without a trail.
'This is the best, I swear it's true,
I glided here, now who are you?'

With every flake, a giggle grows,
As snowmen sprout with goofy poses.
Sticks for arms, they take their stance,
And all the kids join in the dance.

So raise a cup to chilly days,
Where winter's charm brings silly ways.
In crystal lattice, we find our fun,
In nature's art, we all are one!

Sparkling Veils of December

In slippers of snow, we dance like fools,
Chasing the flakes, breaking all the rules.
With hats that are jaunty, and scarves wrapped tight,
We tumble and tumble, oh what a sight!

Hot cocoa spills over, we laugh till we cry,
As snowmen start wobbling, oh me, oh my!
With carrot noses that melt in the sun,
Who knew winter fun could weigh a ton?

Our snowball fight starts, a flurry of glee,
But wait! That's not snow, that's a rogue bumblebee!
With squeals of delight, we dash for the door,
Wishing every winter was never a bore!

So here's to the laughter, the chill in the air,
And all that's fluffy — we haven't a care.
In sparkling veils, let our jesters convene,
In January's grip, we keep it serene!

Glimmering Echoes in the Silence

Whispers of giggles echo through the trees,
As snowflakes descend, giving everyone freeze.
With each crunching step, a symphony forms,
A chorus of chuckles — oh, the silliness warms!

In the hush of the night, we sled down the hills,
With shouts that could rival a thousand thrills.
Our cheeks are like cherries, our noses bright red,
As we glide like penguins on sleds built of bread!

The stars twinkle down, share their laughter with us,
As we launch our snowballs with reckless fuss.
We topple and roll, a frosted embrace,
Giggling so hard — we can't keep the pace!

In this frigid realm where glee intertwines,
We craft our own magic, spun from the pines.
With glimmering echoes that dance in the chill,
Every winter mischief is sure to fulfill!

The Silent Symphony of Winter

In a cloud of snow, we spin and we twirl,
While snowflakes land softly, like diamonds they whirl.
A concert begins with the clinking of ice,
As we sip on our cocoa — oh, isn't it nice?

I spot a fat squirrel preparing to feast,
On leftover crumbs from last week's big feast.
He wiggles and jiggles, a hilarious sight,
In the spotlight of winter's frost-kissed light!

A frostbitten songbird joins the wild troupe,
With a chirp so high, it could make the sun stoop.
As we hoot like owls through this cold winter night,
The silent symphony fills hearts with delight!

Under blankets of snow, we create our own jam,
With hot pies on the stove — oh, what a grand slam!
In this winter's orchestra, joy makes us sway,
United in laughter, we'll dance till the day!

Elfin Echoes in the Snow

In a world made of marshmallows and cream,
The elves skitter by, grinning ear to ear.
With snowflakes for hats and gumdrops for shoes,
They sprinkle the path with giggles and cues.

They dance on the corners, pull pranks on us all,
Then duck in the snow when we come for a brawl.
With candy cane shenanigans, laughter runs wild,
As we race through the flakes, every adult a child!

Through frosty white landscapes, we tumble and play,
While giggling sprites shine in their own special way.
They giggle and chortle, the stars in their eyes,
With stories that tickle like sweet summer fries!

So here's to the laughter, snow flurries of fun,
We'll chase after echoes till the season is done.
For in elfin echoes, chilly giggles abound,
In the fluffiest snow, our joy can be found!

Fantasia Beneath a Frosty Canopy

Under the trees, snowflakes twirl,
A chilly dance, a winter whirl.
Squirrels slide, with grace they boast,
While frozen nuts they laugh and toast.

Icicles hang like frozen spears,
A battlefield of frozen tears.
The rabbits hop, wearing hats quite fine,
In their frosty world, they toast with wine!

Snowmen grin with buttoned cheer,
And whisper secrets per snowy leer.
While birds wear scarves and tweet so loud,
"Now that's a look," says the frozen crowd!

So dance we must, where frost may gleam,
In this comical winter dream.
With laughter ringing, hearts swell wide,
In the chilly fun, we all abide.

The Lure of Frost-Kissed Secrets

In a garden wrapped in wintry lace,
The carrots whisper: "Give us space!"
Snowflakes giggle as they flutter down,
While the hedgehogs wear a frosty crown.

Beneath the frost, the secrets sleep,
As penguins waddle in a freezing leap.
The turnips chuckle, "We're not alone!"
As snowflakes dance on their icy throne.

The world is quiet, yet full of jest,
Each chilly breeze a playful quest.
"Is that a snowman or a mighty sage?"
As winter plays upon the stage.

With frosty nibbles and chill delights,
We hold our breath for sparkling sights.
In the twilight's shimmer, laughter blooms,
In this icy realm, joy swiftly zooms.

Veils of Winter's Enchantment

Frosty blankets cover the ground,
Where cheeky mice scurry round.
The shadows play hide and seek,
As sunny spirits begin to peek.

A bear in boots, what a scene!
Sipping cocoa, he looks quite keen.
Snowballs fly in friendly fights,
While winter wraps us in pure delights.

Icicles dangle, twinkling bright,
In the giggle-filled winter night.
The snowy owls hoot a tune,
As frosty fairies dance by the moon.

With every chill, the laughter grows,
In this realm where cold wind blows.
So gather 'round, let joy take flight,
In the realm of white, what a sight!

Elusive Blooms of the Cold

Petals hidden 'neath icy shrouds,
They giggle softly to chilly crowds.
With frost on noses, they blush and sway,
"Who said flowers can't have fun today?"

Snowflakes are laughter in each swirl,
A winter's party, in a frosty whirl.
Swaying bushes whisper with glee,
"Look at us, as silly as can be!"

Bright colors peek through frozen white,
A rainbow hiding, what a sight!
With frosty wigs on each tiny grin,
They beckon everyone to join in.

So frolic we must in this playful chill,
As magic unfolds with every thrill.
In elusive blooms of winter's play,
Laughter and joy are here to stay.

Frozen Echoes in the Heart of Nature

In the woods where giggles roam,
Trees wear coats of chilly foam.
Squirrels dance in icy shoes,
Chasing shadows, laughing blues.

An owl hiccups, takes a glance,
At the rabbits' frozen dance.
Snowflakes swirl like silly hats,
Nature's circus, just for cats.

Pinecones juggle with frostied cheer,
As winter laughs, drawing near.
The brook sings to the icy stones,
While fishes hear it, dance like clones.

Nature's jokes grow louder, spry,
As snowflakes twirl and vapors fly.
So let us join this merry play,
In the woods of winter's sway.

The Twilight of Crystal Leaves

Leaves like jewels hang from trees,
Whispering secrets with the breeze.
A fox in boots takes a quick stroll,
Complaining of the winter's toll.

The sun dips slow, a golden tease,
As chipmunks don their warmest fleece.
Snowmen wink with carrot grins,
Plotting mischief, where it begins.

Icicles hang like bright chandeliers,
Making melodies that melt our fears.
A crow tells jokes to frosty pines,
While rabbits munch on snowflake lines.

In the twilight, giggles swell,
Beneath the frosty, frozen spell.
We dance 'neath stars, in blankets warm,
Laughing, living through the charm.

Whispers of Winter's Veil

In the hush of winter's night,
Snowflakes giggle in the light.
A tree with laughter starts to sway,
While critters plot their fun display.

A moose wears snow as fluffy hats,
While squirrels juggle snowy brats.
Snowballs fly like laughter loud,
Proving winter's quite the crowd.

Twinkling stars in icy skies,
Invite the owls to share their sighs.
While rabbits host a wild, bold show,
In the land where the cold winds blow.

Whispers travel through the trees,
Echoing secrets as they freeze.
Nature's laugh, a frosty tune,
As we dance beneath the moon.

Enchanted Icicles

Icicles dangle, winking bright,
As snowmen chuckle in delight.
The frosty ground is a comical stage,
Where winter's antics uncage the rage.

A penguin pair takes a twirl,
On frozen ponds, they start to whirl.
"Watch out!" shouts the snowflake crew,
As laughter echoes, cold and true.

Cocoa brews in cups of cheer,
While frosty ghosts whisper near.
Branches creak with playful sounds,
Adding to nature's merry rounds.

In this land of crisp white dreams,
Life's a party, or so it seems.
Frosted wonders, full of glee,
Dance with us, wild and free.

Glistening Leaves of Imagination

In the forest, giggles grow,
Where frozen leaves put on a show.
They dance with glee in the winter light,
Waving at squirrels in sheer delight.

A carrot-nosed snowman stands tall,
Cracking jokes, making snowflakes fall.
The trees are whispering, quite absurd,
About a rabbit who dreamt of a bird.

Icicles hang like chandeliers,
Boasting tales of frozen beers.
They clink and clatter in the breeze,
Sharing secrets as they freeze.

Let's jump in puddles that glitter bright,
Splashing around in wintry white.
With every slip, a hearty cheer,
Winter's laughter is always near.

Shimmering Shadows Amidst the Chill

Shadows dance in playful ways,
Chasing moonbeams on snowy days.
A friendly raccoon dons a hat,
And tips it low, just like a cat.

The owls hoot jokes in the trees,
As frostbite tickles the chilly breeze.
A playful fox with a scarf so bold,
Tells winter tales that never get old.

Snowflakes twirl like silly dreams,
Giggling as they glide in streams.
In the moonlight, shadows come alive,
Turning each frosty prank to jive.

A snowball fight breaks the serene,
Laughter echoes, so fresh and clean.
With each throw and each falling flake,
The world is alive, for joy's own sake.

Laced with Hoarfrost Hope

A tree in the yard wears a crystal crown,
Each branch adorned as if it won a gown.
It sways and shakes, a frosty tease,
Beckoning us to join with ease.

A bunny hops in sparkling snow,
Leaps and bounds like it's put on a show.
With whiskers twitching from the chill,
It laughs and rolls, such a frosty thrill.

The sun peeks out, but the cold won't budge,
Even the icicles seem to begrudge.
But there's a warmth in this frosted land,
That tickles the toes, forever unplanned.

The snowman smirks with eyes of coal,
Sharing secrets as he takes his stroll.
In winter's grip, let's not be blue,
For every laugh is a frosty cue.

Ethereal Patterns on Glassy Wings

A butterfly flaps with a frosty flair,
Landing softly on the winter air.
It giggles softly, just like a breeze,
Colorful wings that freeze with ease.

The penguins waddle in a row,
Playing limbo in the fluffy snow.
One slips and falls with a funny grunt,
As laughter echoes from the snowy front.

Sparkling crystals on every face,
Chasing each other in a playful race.
The frosty patterns swirl and spin,
Creating smiles where joy begins.

The chilly wind sings a silly tune,
Under the shimmering, frosty moon.
With every flop and every glide,
In this wintry world, we take a ride.

Veins of Ice in Wooded Echoes

In a forest of giggles, the trees wear a grin,
A dance-off of shadows, let the fun begin!
Squirrels in sunglasses, tapping their toes,
With frost on their noses, they steal all the shows.

A deer holds a mic, it sings out of tune,
While rabbits in bowties play jazz to the moon.
Snowflakes as confetti, they fall, oh so bright,
As creatures dressed fancy join in for the night.

Moonlit Traces of Frost

Beneath the glow, a moon made of cheese,
The critters all gather, doing just as they please.
Frogs wear top hats, they croak out the beat,
While owls hoot in chorus, on their dancing feet.

Puppies in jackets slip over the snow,
Making snow angels while putting on a show.
Chasing their tails, they twirl in a song,
Nature's own jesters, all merry and strong.

Nature's Frozen Palette

Painted leaves hanging like ornaments bright,
Even the snowflakes look ready to bite.
A caterpillar sneezes, breaks into fits,
As snowmen applaud with their stick-arm wits.

The river wears diamonds, the trees are in lace,
Silly ice sculptures make funny grimace.
Each branch is a canvas, each twig a new stroke,
Where winter's a jester, and laughter's no joke.

Frosted Whispers Under Starlit Sky

Under a blanket of twinkling delight,
The stars tell their secrets with all of their might.
A moose wears a crown made of snow and of light,
While the bunnies hop round, oh what a sight!

The night breathes a chuckle, it echoes so clear,
As chipmunks throw snowballs, with nothing to fear.
Giggles in breezes, they dance through the trees,
A party in winter, but make sure to freeze!

Shadows in the Frost

In winter's grip, the shadows play,
They dance and twirl in a quirky way.
Frogs wear scarves, the owls are wise,
While squirrels juggle snacks under icy skies.

The trees wear glitter, a shiny coat,
Rabbits in mittens, ready to gloat.
Snowflakes whisper jokes, soft and light,
As laughter echoes through the chilly night.

A snowman tells tales of warm sunny days,
While snowdrops giggle in white, frosty bays.
The chill is funny, it brings a cheer,
As shadows frolic, brightening the drear.

So let's embrace the cold, my friend,
With laughter and joy that never quite ends.
In shadows of frost, fun's never lost,
Just grab your cocoa, and laugh at the cost!

The Whispering Woods at Dusk

In the woods where whispers creep,
Trees giggle softly, secrets to keep.
Owles in pajamas hoot out loud,
While rabbits hop by, feeling proud.

The bushes gossip, "Do you hear?
That squirrel just tripped—oh dear, oh dear!"
The shadows chuckle, tickling the night,
Dancing in moonbeams, what a sight!

Frosty patterns make the ground laugh,
As snowflakes play tag, mapping their path.
"Hey! Don't eat yellow snow!" they tease,
Echoing laughter through frosty trees.

At dusk, the woods come alive with cheer,
A whimsical world where giggles appear.
So join the revel, leave worries aside,
In the woods at dusk, let fun be your guide!

Whimsy of a Breathless Chill

A breathless chill tickles your nose,
While penguins waddle in fanciful clothes.
Snowflakes spin like ballerinas in flight,
As the cold air sparkles, shimmering bright.

Icicles dangle, sharp as a joke,
While polar bears wear hats, look at them poke!
The frosty wind sings a merry tune,
As winter's fun blossoms under the moon.

Let's build a snow fort, not just a mound,
With cushions and snacks that we all have found.
Frosty mischief calls for a giggle or two,
As we lose ourselves in this chilly view.

So breathe in the chill, let laughter ignite,
In this wintry whimsy, everything feels right.
As we cherish each moment, together we thrill,
In the depth of a winter, a breathless chill!

Latticework of Ice and Leaf

A lattice of ice wraps the ground with glee,
Each twig a masterpiece, can't you see?
Leaves whisper stories, frozen and bold,
In patterns of magic, twinkling like gold.

The critters prance in a shimmery show,
Beneath the glistening frost, almost aglow.
With squirrels on skates and ducks in a line,
The giggles grow louder; oh how they shine!

Let's make a toast with hot cocoa in hand,
As ice sculptures rise like a sparkling band.
The garden does chuckle, "I'm cooler than you,"
As each frosty leaf plays peek-a-boo!

So dance through the snow with a skip and a hop,
In a world where laughter will never stop.
For in this lattice of ice and leaf,
Joy blooms in winter, beyond all belief!

Silvery Dreams Beneath the Snow

In a land where snowflakes giggle and spin,
The squirrels wear scarves as they frolic and grin.
Trees, dressed like penguins, waddle and sway,
While the rabbits hold snowball fights every day.

Icicles shimmer like knights in a fight,
Chasing shadows that dance in the pale moonlight.
The snowmen gossip with frosty delight,
Telling tales of the chill that just isn't right.

When snow makes the world a glittering scene,
The owls roll their eyes; it's so rarely serene.
Yet laughter rings out, oh what a sweet sound,
In this chilly kingdom where fun knows no bound.

So pour out some cocoa, let troubles take flight,
Join the snowflake ballet beneath twinkling light.
For in this cool palace, where laughter will flower,
Every snowy moment gives joy by the hour.

The Dance of Frosted Whispers

Little flakes tumble in a dizzying swirl,
They whisper sweet secrets as they twirl and twirl.
The pine trees stand silent, their branches aglow,
While snowflakes giggle, giving nature a show.

Bunnies in boots chase their tails with delight,
As penguins in bowties prepare for a night.
The chill on their cheeks is like cherry on cake,
With each frosty giggle, the whole world will shake!

The moon winks at clouds with a frosty grin,
While icicles dangle like they're in a spin.
Every snowdrift grumbles, "Why are we so blue?"
But laughter erupts as they dance on cue!

So gather your mittens and join in the fun,
For frosty whispers have only begun.
Let laughter ring out in the sparkling night,
In this silly winter wonderland of light.

Hidden Worlds in Crystal Lattice

Beneath icy layers, where secrets may hide,
Are snowflake castles where chilly elves bide.
They sip on hot cocoa with marshmallows bright,
Donning hats made of icicles, oh what a sight!

Tiny snow creatures build homes with a laugh,
Creating a marvel in this crystal path.
When snowmen parade in their frosty attire,
The world's full of magic—it's quite the quire!

With each little footstep, a crunch and a cheer,
They giggle and wiggle, spreading warmth, never fear.
A snow angel trails with wings wide and free,
While the squirrels take selfies from the top of a tree.

So run through the drifts, and leap with delight,
For winter's a stage where laughter takes flight.
In each hidden corner of this gleaming expanse,
May your heart find the joy in the wintertime dance!

When Winter Paints with a Brush of Ice

With an icy brush, winter colors the trees,
Painting snowmen with hats that sway in the breeze.
Penguins in top hats slide down icy hills,
While snowflakes sprinkle some chilly good thrills.

Frosted pancakes for breakfast serve up quite a treat,
As squirrels sip smoothies that taste like a feat.
The rabbits play chess while the owls referee,
In this whimsical realm, you can laugh with glee!

A giggling brook bubbles beneath the gray mist,
Making snowball proposals in frosty twist.
When arctic breezes decide to join the play,
The dance party starts with each winter display.

So cuddle up warm with a smile on your face,
In this wild snowy season, there's always a place.
Where laughter ignites, and whimsy is rife,
When winter paints joy, it brings joy to life!

Tapestry of Icy Fantasies

Under the ice, the ferns dance bright,
Pretending to take flight in the night.
With whispers of jokes in the chilly air,
They giggle and twirl without a care.

Snowflakes flutter like laughter, oh dear,
As chilly critters gather near.
In the madness of winter's tight grip,
The ferns plot mischief, a frosty trip.

Dreams in a Glacial Garden

In the garden where the cool winds blow,
Silly sprites hop, putting on a show.
They wear tiny mittens, each slightly askew,
Chasing their shadows, what a silly crew!

A penguin in shades takes a regal stance,
Declaring a snowball delightfully by chance.
With laughter and snow, they dance on the ground,
In dreams where the frosty giggles abound.

Mysteries Wrapped in Frost

Whispers of secrets lurk in the frost,
Where silly ideas might just get lost.
A rabbit's half-twist, a snowman's sneer,
They share hidden jokes that only they hear.

Covered in ice, the landscape's a tease,
With ticklish snowflakes that flutter and freeze.
Every corner holds a giggle or two,
In this wonderland where laughter is due.

Constellations of Frozen Ferns

In the starry night under frost's embrace,
Ferns giggle softly, plotting their race.
Starlight twinkles as they swirl and sway,
Who knew snowflakes could dance in such play?

Each blade of grass holds a whimsical tale,
A frosty adventure with a giggle-filled trail.
With ice as their canvas, they sketch in delight,
A cosmos of chuckles that sparkles so bright.

A Waltz in the Frosted Glades

In the glades where rabbits dance,
Each hop's a clumsy chance.
Snowflakes swirl in a dizzy spree,
They laugh as branches wave with glee.

Penguins glide with cheerful flair,
Slip and slide without a care.
A snowman winks, his carrot nose,
Is stuck on sideways, just like those.

Squirrels giggle, tails in flight,
Building castles, what a sight!
They toss snowballs in the air,
Then slip and land, with frosty flair.

So let us twirl in icy bliss,
While tasting snow, a frosty kiss.
In glades where laughter fills the sky,
We waltz with grins, both low and high.

Twilight's Breath of Ice

As twilight falls, the world a chill,
A snowman's scarf, he wears with thrill.
His button eyes, a cheeky stare,
Makes even snowflakes pause and care.

The owls hoot jokes from frosty trees,
As critters gather, eager to please.
A game of charades, the stars in tow,
With ice-cold giggles that start to flow.

Snowflakes tickle a polar bear,
Who rolls and tumbles without a care.
His fluffy belly, a winter's joy,
He twirls like a happy, fuzzy toy.

So dance with shadows in icy hues,
With chuckles bright, let joy ensue.
In twilight's grip, our laughter flies,
As stars twinkle through the frosty skies.

The Resplendence of Winter's Grasp

In winter's clutch, the world is bright,
With every breath, a frosty bite.
Penguins prance, a comic scene,
In boots of ice, they slide, and lean.

A snowball fight ensues with cheer,
As frosty warriors gather near.
Chasing tails and rumors swell,
The frost-tinged gossips weave their spell.

Trees in glitter, dressed for fun,
With tiny lights, they've surely won.
Nutcrackers grin with holiday flair,
As snowflakes pile upon their hair.

So join the jam in winter's grasp,
Where laughter hangs and sweet dreams clasp.
Beneath the blanket of sparkling white,
We dance and jest till the morning light.

Fantasia Beneath the Ice

Beneath the ice, the world does glow,
As penguins skate in quite a show.
They twirl and glide with silly spins,
Creating havoc, and cheeky grins.

Frosty fairies with icy wings,
Share all their jokes and winter flings.
They sprinkle giggles like snowflakes bright,
Creating chaos in the moonlight.

A snowcat purrs, with frosty breath,
Chasing shadows, a snowball's death.
In this cold world, not all is glum,
As laughter echoes, the fun is from.

So come and play in this chilly theme,
With frosty laughter and winter's dream.
In a fantastical freeze of fun,
Let's dance until the day is done.

Ethereal Escapades in White

In the garden where whispers play,
Snowflakes tumble, come what may.
Frogs in hats hop on the ground,
Sipping tea without a sound.

Squirrels wear their winter gear,
Dancing round without a fear.
Snowmen gossip, noses bright,
Their carrot jokes are pure delight.

Penguins waddle, flap their wings,
Claiming snow is what joy brings.
In this realm of icy cheer,
Everyone's laughing, never fear!

With each step, a crunch, a slide,
Who's the king of winter pride?
It's the raccoon with a crown,
Rolling through the snowy town!

Serenity of a Frozen Realm

In the stillness where chill prevails,
Gnomes are plotting grand details.
Building castles made of ice,
Decorated with sugar spice.

Hamsters sledding down the hill,
Chasing dreams with such great skill.
Laughter echoes, pure delight,
Underneath the silver light.

Snowflakes flutter, twirl, and glide,
Kittens chase them, full of pride.
Every pounce, a frosty dance,
Even the trees join in the prance!

Here the clouds wear winter hats,
While rabbits dance with other rats.
In this peace, a playful cheer,
Every giggle sparks the year!

Frost-inked Petals on Silence

Petals crunch beneath my feet,
Frosty patterns, oh so neat.
A snail in boots slides with finesse,
While flowerpots don winter dress.

Chickens strut in fuzzy coats,
Doing the cha-cha, claiming votes.
With each chirp, a hearty laugh,
Beneath the chilly photograph.

Icicles sparkle, dripping low,
As penguins put on quite a show.
With flippers flapping, what a sight,
They twirl and whirl in pure delight!

In this world of frozen charms,
Everyone's wrapped in winter arms.
Join the dance, the silly spree,
Where frosty dreams are wild and free!

Underneath the Frozen Carpet

Underneath the fluffy snow,
Secrets hide in winter's glow.
A rabbit's burrow, snug and tight,
Holds a party every night.

Mice dressed up in tiny suits,
Sipping juice from frozen fruits.
With each nibble, giggles rise,
As snowflakes fall from frosty skies.

A bear in pajamas, what a sight!
Snoozing softly, snoring light.
Add a hat and scarf, oh dear,
Frozen dreams bring winter cheer!

In this wonderland of white,
There's mischief brewing, pure delight.
Grab your mittens, let's embark,
On a journey through the spark!

Frost-Covered Reveries

In chilly nooks, the critters do freeze,
Wearing coats of white, they sneeze with ease.
A snowman wiggles, with carrot nose,
Sipping hot cocoa, as winter wind blows.

The squirrel takes selfies, but they all flop,
His tail's in the frame, then it goes plop.
He twirls with a snowball, what a mad sight,
Oh, how he wishes it'd just be a night!

A polar bear slips, and he starts to glide,
On a patch of ice, he cannot abide.
With a belly laugh, he tumbles around,
In a sparkly snowdrift, he's lost and drowned.

Snowflakes fall like confetti, a grand ball,
Each dancing down swiftly, some big, some small.
Laughter breaks out, under the full moon,
As frosty delights make us all feel immune.

The Beauty of Unfurling Ice

Icicles dangle like crooked teeth,
The windows are frosty, we're stuck beneath.
Hot chocolate's bubbling, it's time for a chat,
With marshmallows popping, oh, where's the cat?

Snowballs are flying, a comedic fight,
Even the dog joins, oh, what a sight!
The cat scratches heads, in her fluffy disdain,
As dog wears a snowdrift, oh, what a pain!

The world is a stage, icy dreams unfold,
With penguins in suits, they're brazen and bold.
Dancing on ice, with a slip and a slide,
They spin like ballerinas, in glee they confide.

Through breath of the winter, we giggle and sigh,
As ice paints the earth, in a sparkling high.
Thoughts of spring beckon, with dreams yet to grow,
Yet here, in this chill, we put on our show.

Glacial Dances at Dusk

Amidst the frost, a party so bright,
The owls get down, with all of their might.
They hoot and they flap, with style so grand,
Wearing ice crowns, on a snow-covered land.

The rabbits are twirling, with snowshoe delight,
In fluffy tuxedos, oh, what a sight!
They hop near the lanterns, made from pure ice,
And breakdance with snowflakes — oh, isn't that nice?

As shadows slink low, with giggles and cheer,
Each critter brings laughter, while winter draws near.
Unruly old frost, with a mischievous grin,
Tosses blizzards for fun, that's where the game begins!

A twinkle of stars, the moon gives a wink,
And all of the frostlings join in the link.
With a clap of the paws, and a stomp of the feet,
Winter's wild party can't be beat!

Gossamer Dreams of Winter

On soft, snowy pillows, the children all lay,
As dreams of warm summers begin to play.
They ride on the backs of clouds made of fluff,
Wishing for sunbeams, but the weather's too tough.

Frosty whispers cradle them in a dance,
Where penguins in bowties perform their strange prance.
The tea party's chilly, with icecream galore,
They sip on cool breezes, then beg for some more!

Footsteps crunch softly, in pathways of white,
A yeti sings karaoke, oh, what a fright!
The calendar chuckles, with days cold and brisk,
Reminding us all, it's not time for risk!

And the world spins on, in this whimsical chill,
As snowflakes drift down, like dreams that fulfill.
With hats full of giggles, and mittened small hands,
We stumble through winter, in laughter, we stand.

Frostbite and Folklore

In the garden, snowflakes twirl,
Waving for a winter swirl.
Who knew the carrots wore a hat?
And sang silly songs with the cat?

Chilly gnomes in a line they stand,
Offering tea from a frosty hand.
A snowman's nose took flight one day,
Escaping to join the ice ballet!

Snowmen gossip, their rounds are wide,
Whispering tales of the icy slide.
The squirrels dance in furry suits,
While trying to steal the winter fruits.

With sticky mittens, kids have fun,
As snowballs fly beneath the sun.
And if one lands upon your head,
Just laugh and wear your frosty thread!

The Lament of Winter's Kiss

Oh, winter! You trickster of cold delight,
You tumble us into pure frosty fright.
With frozen windows and snowflakes galore,
You steal my gloves and leave me wanting more!

A snowflake landed right on my nose,
Whispering secrets that nobody knows.
And there went my hat, spun high in the breeze,
As I chased it down like a clumsy, cold tease.

Lemonade's dreams now frozen in time,
I watched in despair as my drink turned to grime.
But hey, catch a snowflake, let's dance with glee,
Together we'll make the best of this spree!

Chilled by your touch, yet I must abide,
Hilarity reigns when I slip and glide.
Oh winter, sweet joker, your pranks never cease,
But in this frozen jest, I find my peace!

Beneath the Icy Mantle

Under blankets of snow, all snug in my bed,
I dream of penguins who dance on their head.
They slip and they slide as they glide on the frost,
In their dapper tuxedos, not caring what's lost!

A hot cocoa fountain erupted, oh dear!
With marshmallows flying, it filled up with cheer.
Now the squirrels are pilfering treats, what a sight!
Tiny bandits in capes on a frosty night.

I called to the frost, "Let us all have some fun!"
Then I slipped on a patch and went down with a run.
The icicles laughed as I flopped like a fish,
Well, if winter's a show, I'll be the main dish!

So grab a warm cocoa, let laughter abound,
With whimsical wonders in circles around.
We'll revel in snowball fights, giggles galore,
In this frosty kingdom, who could ask for more?

Spheres of Frosted Enchantment

Round and round, a snowball whirls,
As voices echo from chilly curls.
A wild snow beast wants to join the fray,
But he's just made of fluff, what a funny display!

Icicles twinkle on each frosty mound,
As giggles and laughter abound all around.
The elves have a party just behind the trees,
With hot cranberry punch and some corny freeze!

Through snowdrifts and warmth, we skate without care,
Waddling like penguins, our antics laid bare.
The winter parade brings joy to all hearts,
But watch out for snowballs, they fly like fine arts!

In this chill-land filled with gleeful mirth,
Every frostbitten moment's a reason for birth.
So join in the magic, don't sit on the side,
In the sphere of winter, let's all giggle and glide!

The Playful Touch of Frost

On windowsills, the chill does dance,
A sprightly jig, a frosty prance.
With scarves and gloves, we face the cold,
Laughs echo loud, as stories unfold.

The ground is white, like spilled ice cream,
We slip and slide, a winter dream.
But in our hearts, there's warmth and cheer,
Snowball fights bring joy each year.

The trees are dressed in crystal wear,
Squirrels dance as if to declare.
"Look at the world, all shiny and bright!"
Nature's joke, a playful sight.

So gather 'round, let laughter ring,
In frosty fun, our hearts take wing.
With every breath, we puff and blow,
Creating clouds in the frosty glow.

Frostbite's Tender Embrace

Oh winter's bite, it tickles my nose,
Bringing forth giggles, not just froze toes.
With snowsuits on, we waddle about,
Like penguins in suits, where's the fun, no doubt?

The air is crisp, our breath puffs wide,
Laughter erupts, we can't run and hide.
With fingers numb, we craft little men,
Who wear silly hats made from old pens.

Each snowflake whispers a quirky tale,
Of how big waffle cones tried to sail.
They landed in marshmallows, stuck and sweet,
Chasing gumdrops down the frosty street.

Behold the snow, a stage on its own,
Where clumsy dancers never feel alone.
In chilly whispers, we find the grace,
Of laughter shared in this frozen place.

Luminous Ferns in the Snow

Under moonlight, the ferns shine bright,
Dressed in silver, a winter delight.
They wiggle and jive, a shimmering band,
With giggles that echo across the land.

A rabbit hops in a fluffy ballet,
While critters chuckle, it's party day!
Frosted leaves giggle, 'What fun we bring!'
As snowflakes dance, and winter birds sing.

They twirl like dancers in frosty attire,
Sprinkled with stardust, they never tire.
"Catch me if you can!" shouts a spry little cat,
Who leaps and fluffs, in a frosty spat.

So come join the fun, in this chilly glow,
Where laughter blooms in the frosty snow.
With radiant ferns and whispers of cheer,
Winter's enchanting, no need for fear!

Hypnotic Traces of Winter's Kiss

Winter comes in with a cheeky smile,
Leaving frosty traces in playful style.
Join the parade of snowflakes that twirl,
As kids chase their dreams in a dreamy whirl.

With mittens on, we stumble and slide,
Snowball battles become the pride.
A funny sight as we all freeze,
While flurries fall down like sneaky bees.

On icy ponds, we skate and spin,
With all of our friends, let the fun begin!
In our furry coats, we slap and clap,
Making snow angels in a frosty lap.

Embrace the chill; wear laughter bright,
As winter teases with sheer delight.
Behold its magic, pure and sweet,
In frosty frolics, life feels complete!

www.ingramcontent.com/pod-product-compliance
Lightning Source LLC
Chambersburg PA
CBHW072140200426
43209CB00051B/190